Name

Teacher

School

AF604144

Learning goal: To improve knowledge of the alphabet in Victorian Modern Cursive script

Success criteria:

- I can write all lower-case and capital letters of the alphabet in Victorian Modern Cursive.
- I can write all lower-case and capital letters of the alphabet in Victorian Modern Cursive legibly, using appropriate slope, spacing and size.

Are you ready to write?

Posture

Ensure your feet are flat on the floor and you are sitting well back in the chair.

Paper position

left-handed

Hold the paper with your non-writing hand.

right-handed

Pencil grip

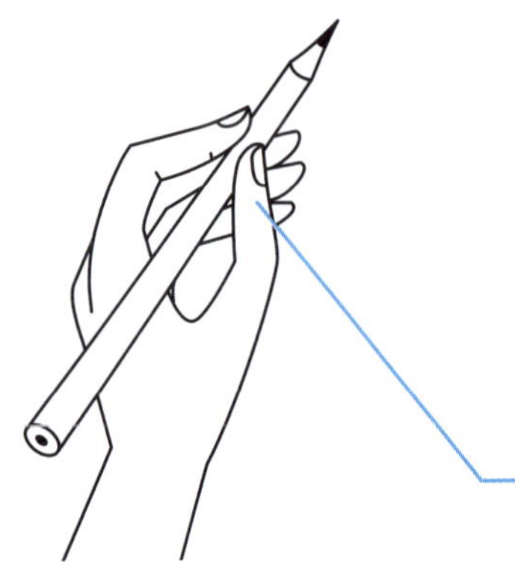

Hold your pen or pencil with one finger on top of the barrel.

Support the barrel with your thumb.

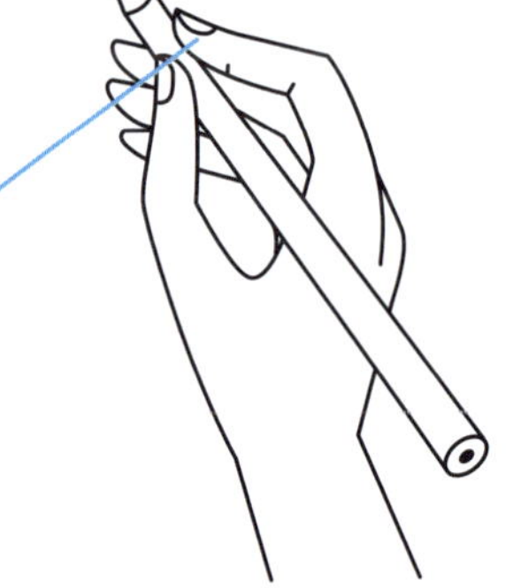

left-handed

right-handed

Unjoined letters

Revise your unjoined letters.

a b c d e f g h i j k l m n o p q r s t u v w x y z

Copy the words below in unjoined letters. Choose three words and mark the starting point of each letter with a coloured dot.

mystery

unsolved puzzling alien time travel unexplained

crop circles mythical creatures investigations believe

sceptic disappearance unusual occurrence Sasquatch

questions lazy cockpit flicker exit unknown

unidentified flying object journey fearful research

truth evidence Abominable Snowman six

Using some of the words from above, write a sentence about mysteries. Ensure that your sentence contains every letter of the alphabet. Use the alphabet at the top of the page to tick off each letter as you use it.

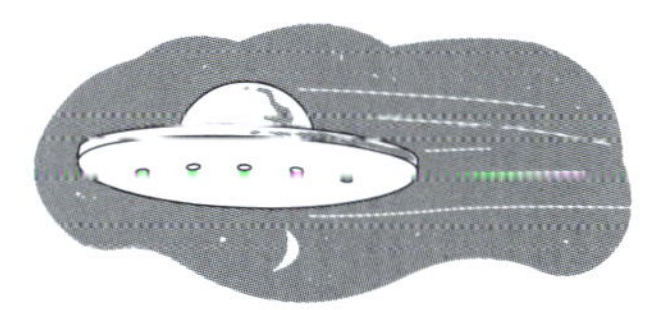

Copy the text.

Crop circles are geometric patterns that mysteriously appear in crop fields. They are flattened areas in cereal crops. A cereologist is someone who studies crop circles. Though cereologists acknowledge that some crop circles are human-made, most believe that many of the patterns are created by time travellers or aliens.

Trace and repeat these patterns. Complete the rows.

Mysterious crop circles

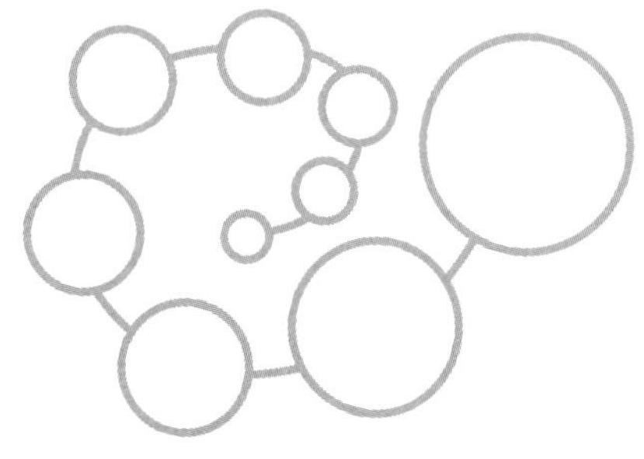

Letter groups

Write each letter of the alphabet in the correct group. Use the alphabet at the bottom of the page as a checklist.

Downstroke letters (4)	Closed anti-clockwise letters (5)
Open anti-clockwise letters (9)	**Clockwise letters (8)**

Look at the sentence below, then:

- Underline the downstroke letters.
- Place a dot above the closed anti-clockwise letters.
- Place a tick above the open anti-clockwise letters.
- Circle the clockwise letters.

Some people say that the first crop circles were
found in Tully, a small town in Queensland, where
a farmer claimed to see a flying saucer rise up
and fly away, leaving a circular area of flattened
grass behind.

Copy the sentence above. Take special care with the starting points and movement of each letter.

a b c d e f g h i j k l m n o p q r s t u v w x y z

Capital letters

Copy the capital letters, then mark the starting point of each letter with a coloured dot. Remember, if you are left-handed, your starting point might be different from right-handers.

A B C D E F G H I J K L M N O P Q R S T U

V W X Y Z

Rewrite these sentences, using capital letters in the appropriate places.

ufo is an abbreviation for 'unidentified flying object'.

many spectacular crop circles have appeared in wiltshire,

in southern england.

dr horace drew is a well-known cereologist who believes

crop circles are messages from aliens.

'war of the worlds' is a famous science fiction novel by

author h. g. wells about a conflict between humankind

and an extraterrestrial race.

my dad says, 'i'm a sceptic – i doubt that aliens exist'.

Numerals

Revise your numerals.

0 1 2 3 4 5 6 7 8 9 10 11 12 13 14 15 16 17 18 19 20

The typical diameter of a crop circle is between 50 and 500 metres. Write each numeral and numeral name.

5 — 5 five

50

500

5000

50 000

500 000

5 000 000

Complete the table.

500 050	
15 500	
	five thousand and fifteen
	five million, fifty thousand and five
50 050	
555	

Write the number from the table above that is more than six hundred thousand, in numerals and words.

Speed loops from clockwise finishers

Speed loops help you to write faster and with fluency.

ga je yo zi

loop crosses here

Speed loops from g, j, y and z cross at the baseline. Make the loop about half the width of a letter.

Copy these letter pairs and words with speed loops from 'g'.

go gr gl gu gh gi ge ga go gr gl gu gh gi ge

glory grass ground ageless large glove glad

green largest giggle ginger again gate general

Copy these letter pairs and words with speed loops from 'j'.

ja je ji jo ju ja je ji jo ju ja je ji jo ju

jaguar jackal joint joke jeans banjo enjoy

adjust rejoice injury subject judge majority

Copy these letter pairs and words with speed loops from 'y'.

yo yr ye ya yi yu yl yt yp yr yo ye ya yi

yellow yam yoghurt yacht myth yeast

typewriter tyre youthful year lyrics mayonnaise

Copy these letter pairs and words with speed loops from 'z'.

za ze zi zl zo zz zy za ze zi zl zo zz zy

zebra zoom zip zoo hazelnut dazzling maze

blizzard bizarre pretzel frozen pizza hazard

journeying

Remember: no speed loop is needed if a word ends in g, j, y or z.

Copy.

yearning young gravity majority blitz topaz

abuzz fuzzy amazing zany flying baby

Speed loops to ascenders

loop crosses here → ch al

A speed loop to b, h, k or l crosses at the height of a body letter.

Remember: a speed loop is not needed if b, h, k or l is at the beginning of a word.

Copy these letter pairs and words with speed loops to 'b'.

mb ob ub bb rb ab mb ob ub bb rb ab

bathtub rhubarb disturb lamb superb absorb

Copy these letter pairs and words with speed loops to 'h'.

ph th sh gh ch oh ph th sh gh ch oh

photograph think show shout chess shower touch

Copy these letter pairs and words with speed loops to 'k'.

ak ek nk rk sk ok ck ak ek nk rk sk ok ck

acknowledge knock unmask shrink attack bark

Copy these letter pairs and words with speed loops to 'l'.

gl pl ul al ol ll tl rl gl pl ul al ol ll tl rl

glitter please bully rally holiday twirl plaster

Speed loops to 'f'

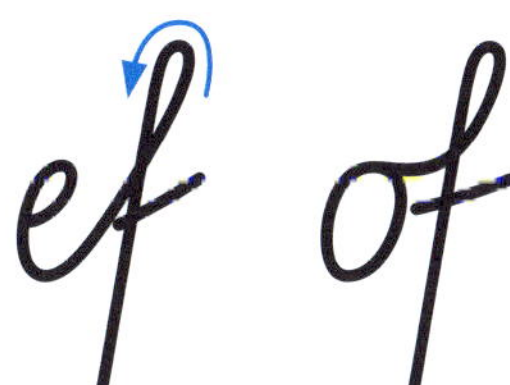

Use a speed loop to join diagonally and horizontally to 'f'. Extend the exit of the previous letter to form a loop.

Copy these words with speed loops to 'f'.

wolf self brief chef leaf relief reef

proof hoof aloof roof aloof surf scarf

unidentified

When 'f' is in the middle of a word, lift your pen and use the crossbar to join to the next letter.

Copy these words with 'f' in the middle of a word.

afraid waterfall awful after loft sift lifeless

left before defeat tofu conflict fluffy prefer

forever

Remember: no loop is needed when 'f' is at the beginning of a word.

Copy these words beginning with 'f'.

field fascination flattened forward found first

flying future fair fear foraging fantasy fully

Speed loops from descenders to ascenders

Speed loops from descenders to ascenders can be tricky. Sweep up diagonally from the tail speed loop to form a loop to the ascender.

Copy these letter pairs.

gb gl gh gf yb yl yf yh zl gb gl gh gf yb yl

Copy these words with speed loops from descenders to ascenders.

bright light playful sightings through glory globe

glitter glimpse puzzling Bigfoot wrongful sightings

midnight brighten airtight ghost rugby longbow

Copy the sentences and underline the joins from descenders to ascenders. Then use some of the words above to create your own 'I wonder' question.

I wonder ...

Is lightning bright enough to see from space?

If an alien smuggled a cow into space, would

anybody notice?

Practising speed loops

Rewrite the text in cursive. Take special care to add speed loops correctly where required.

The majority of UFO sightings are basically identified as having ordinary explanations. These include:

- aircraft lights
- flocks of birds
- kites
- flares (flashes of brilliant light used as signals)
- lights used for beach and land searches
- bright stars and meteors
- helium balloons
- unusual phenomena, such as ball lightning.

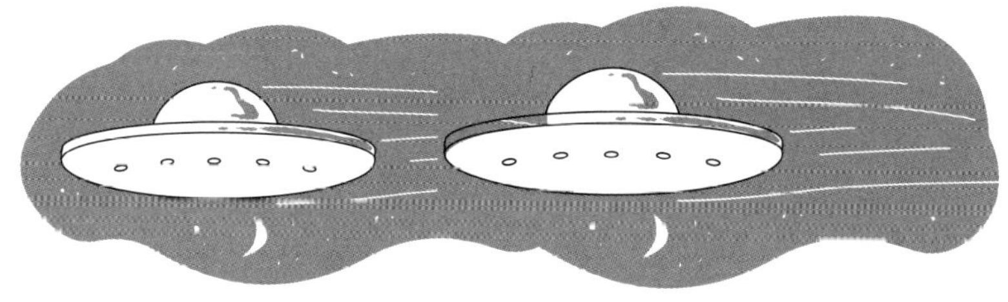

Copy the text, paying careful attention to your speed loops.

On that day in April, 1966, I remember being on the school oval with my friend, Annie. We were students of Westall High School, in the suburb of Clayton South, in Melbourne. Like many of our fellow students, we witnessed three balloon-like objects hovering above the ground. Afterwards, there was a circle of flattened grass left behind, about 5 metres in diameter. I believe the circle was burnt the next day by army officers testing an experimental aircraft. It was such a strange event that I still remember it quite clearly today.

(Fictional recount based on real events)

get.ga/PMWA190

Solving riddles can be good practice for deciphering clues in mysteries, and also good fun. Rewrite the riddles below in cursive, adding speed loops where appropriate.

1. What is so delicate that saying its name breaks it?

2. You live in a place where half the year is warm but the other half is freezing. You find a lake with a small island and decide to build a fort there for you to go with your friends. Your parents give you some planks of wood and a hammer and nails. You don't have a boat or a plane, and the wood is too heavy to carry while swimming. How can you get the materials across to the island to build your fort?

3. Arabella throws a ball as hard as she can. It comes back to her, even though nobody else touches it. How can you explain this?

Match each numbered riddle above with an answer.

She tosses it straight up.

Wait until the lake freezes in winter.

Silence.

Copy the text, taking care with your speed loops.

Is it possible there's life beyond planet Earth? It is a question that has fascinated scientists, who have been hopeful about finding proof for decades. There have certainly been many hoaxes. Aircraft lights, kites and bright stars have been reported as proof that another form of life is trying to contact humans. Some sightings have been so bizarre that a project called 'Breakthrough Listen', which uses powerful telescopes to search for signs of unidentified life, was funded.

Peer review

Ask your partner to give you some feedback on how well you wrote the text above. Ask them to notice how well you formed your speed loops.

2 stars (two things you did well)

☆ ______________________________

☆ ______________________________

1 wish (a way for you to improve)

____

____

Diagonal joins

45° angle

A diagonal join is fast and direct. Extend the exit flick of the first letter on a 45° angle to join to the next letter.

Copy these letter pairs with diagonal joins.

ai ce du ee hi ie ke lu me no ti

ue ci ei ar us he cr le ne is ar an de

Underline the diagonal joins in the following words, then copy the words.

series answer inhabited triangles visible double

beautiful hundreds importantly increased statue

massive implements carefully ceremonial similar

legends complete stonework competition heavily

hidden iconic monolith volcano mysterious

Which of these letter pairs would form a diagonal join in cursive? Circle.

ng em pu re on er ea im an ra le et

Prove your answers by writing all the letter pairs in cursive.

Diagonal joins to 'x' and 'z'

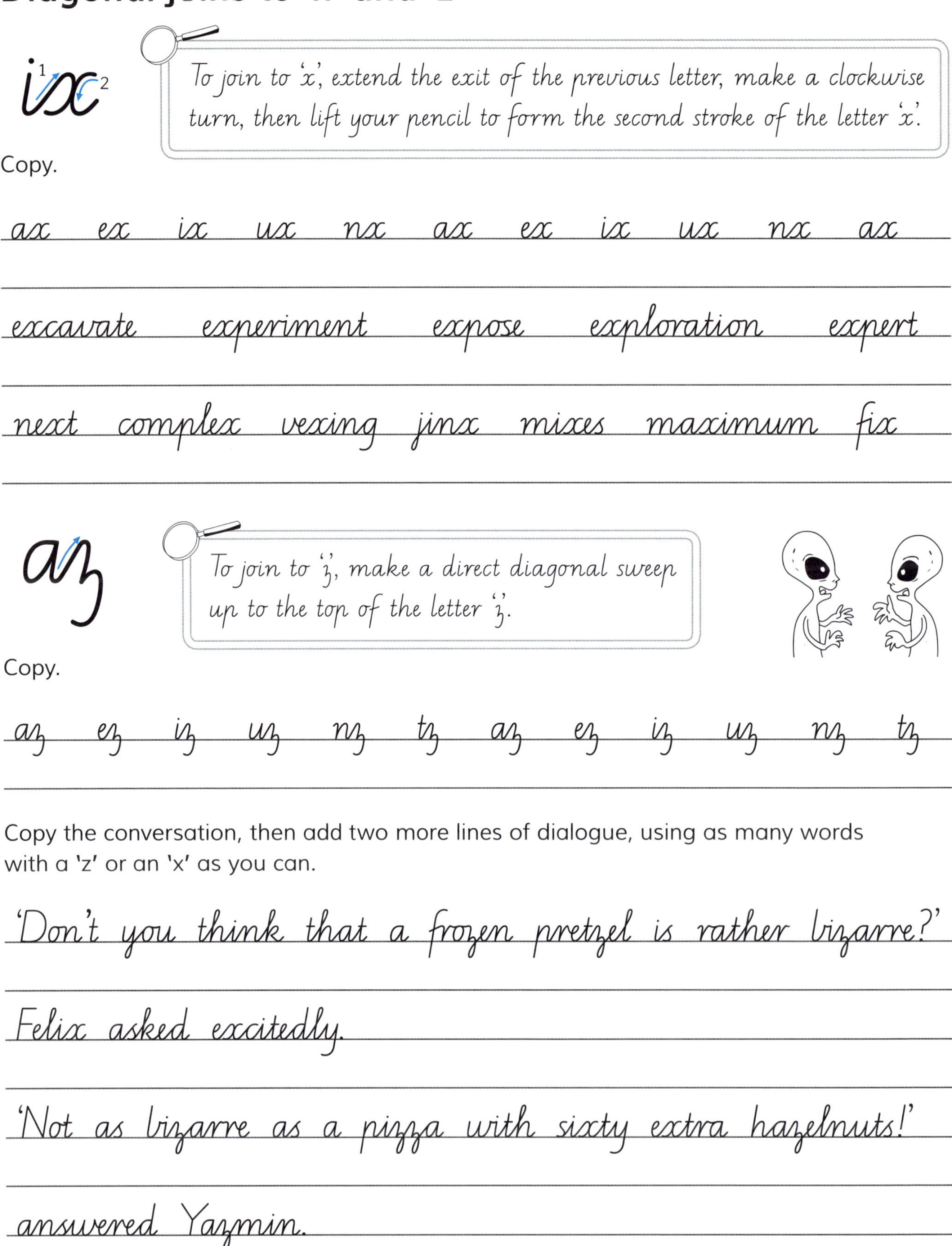

ix

To join to 'x', extend the exit of the previous letter, make a clockwise turn, then lift your pencil to form the second stroke of the letter 'x'.

Copy.

ax ex ix ux nx ax ex ix ux nx ax

excavate experiment expose exploration expert

next complex vexing jinx mixes maximum fix

az

To join to 'z', make a direct diagonal sweep up to the top of the letter 'z'.

Copy.

az ez iz uz nz tz az ez iz uz nz tz

Copy the conversation, then add two more lines of dialogue, using as many words with a 'z' or an 'x' as you can.

'Don't you think that a frozen pretzel is rather bizarre?'

Felix asked excitedly.

'Not as bizarre as a pizza with sixty extra hazelnuts!'

answered Yazmin.

Diagonal joins from 'q'

qu

Remember: 'q' doesn't need a speed loop to join to 'u'.

Copy.

qu qu qu qu qu qu qu qu

Copy the text, paying careful attention to joins from 'q' to 'u'.

Bigfoot is also known as Sasquatch. Sasquatch means 'hairy giant' according to some Indigenous North American legends. People have frequently undertaken quests to find the unique ape-like creature, but no one has succeeded in capturing their quarry, and no one has found its body. Bigfoot is described as being quite tall, from 2 to 2.75 metres. Some say it has brown, black, red or white fur. Its large feet are said to be about 56 centimetres long.

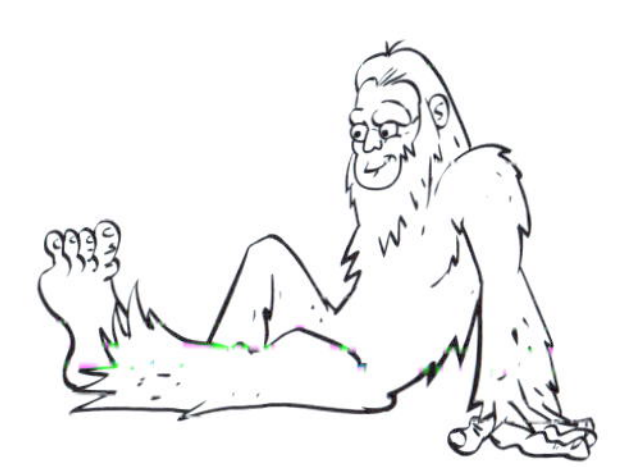

ISBN: 9780170424080

Diagonal joins from 's'

si

Remember to speed up your handwriting by joining from the letter 's'. Retrace along the bottom of the letter.

Copy these letter pairs and words.

sa se si so su sc sn sm sq st sy sp sr

sphere test sceptic deepest straight snow

suspicious story sightings songs disappear

Copy the text, taking care with your joins from 's'.

Throughout history and to this day, strange objects in the sky, monster sightings, peculiar disappearances and other unusual phenomena have captured the public's imagination. People love to speculate and discuss theories in their search for the truth. For some, solving a mystery is like completing a puzzle.

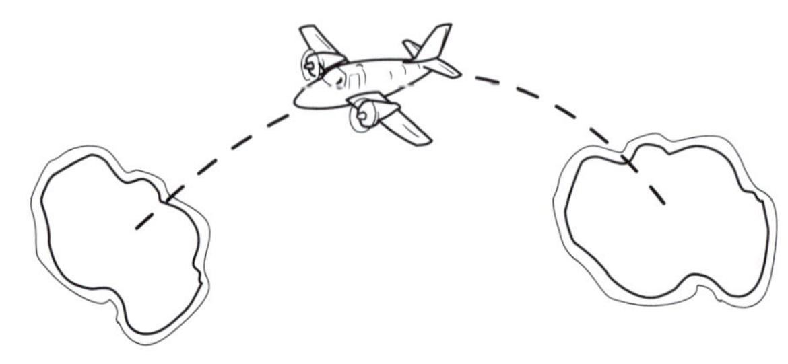

ISBN: 9780170424080

Diagonal joins to 's'

as

> When joining diagonally to 's', modify the shape of your 's' so there is less to retrace.

Copy these letter pairs and words.

as cs ds es is ks ls ms ns ts

case recognise visible existed mysterious

splashes ease monster lakes causes necessary

Copy the text, taking care with your diagonal joins to 's'.

The case of the Loch Ness monster is most mysterious.
Some claim the creature definitely exists and the splashes
it causes are easily visible on the surface of the lake.
Others argue that sightings of the monster have been
comprehensively disproved. They say that no more
investigation is necessary and it is time to close the case.

get.ga/PMWA191

ISBN: 9780170424080

Diagonal joins and speed loops

loop crosses here

ub af

When making a diagonal join to an ascender, make sure the loop crosses at the same height as the top of a body letter.

Copy these letter pairs.

ab cb eb ib lb mb nb ub

ah ch eh ih uh ak ck ek ik

lk mk nk uk al cl el il ll

ml nl pl tl af ef if lf mf uf

Copy these words, taking care with your diagonal joins to ascenders.

circles alien planets travellers include safe

elaborate usually researchers likely specific

weightless unidentified believe clues half

aftermath afraid spacecraft life comfort

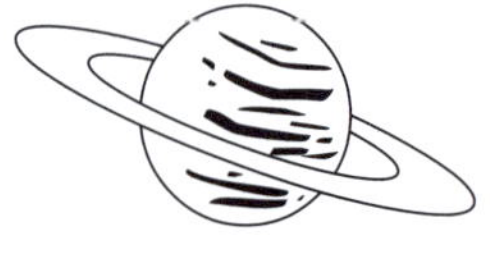
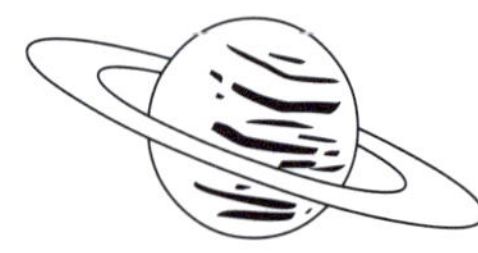

Convert the following words to cursive, taking care with your diagonal joins to ascenders.

unknown subjects claimed about general cycle

belief false closing developed bubbles effective

whales unknown real scientific original explain

circular paranormal sceptical after self effort

Write sentences using the words below, in cursive. Take special care with your diagonal joins. Can you also include other words with diagonal joins to 'f' in your sentences?

unafraid spacecraft confused after belief afar

Self-assessment: Diagonal joins

Copy the text. Remember to be careful with your diagonal joins.

I had heard of the legend of the Yeti before I embarked
on my trip to Nepal. I knew that some people claimed
to have seen a Yeti, and even taken grainy photographs.
I had heard about the large footprints seen in the snow.
What I was not prepared for, while taking a walk,
was a sighting in the distance of what could have
been a Yeti. The creature appeared to be taller than
me, with a shaggy, bent, ape-like back. I was not
frightened, but curious, my feet frozen to the spot. I
made a mental note to try to find footprints later.

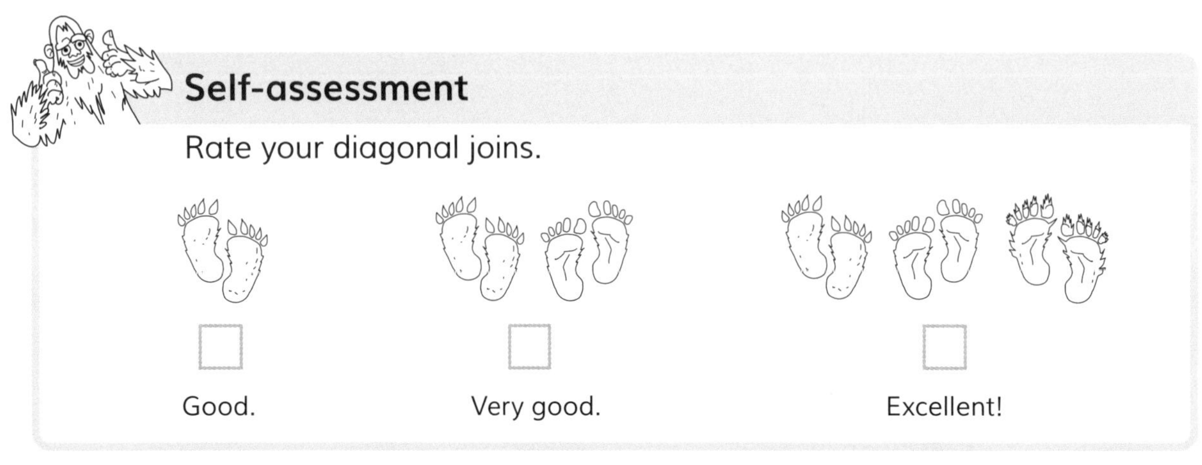

get.ga/PMWA192

Touch joins

Touch joins are diagonal joins to a, c, d, g and q. Touch joins help fluency by reducing how much you need to retrace.

Make a high exit, then lift your pen and drop in the second letter. The dropped-in letter touches the exit of the letter before it.

Copy these letter pairs with touch joins.

ea nc nd ig aq ia ec id ug iq ua ic ag

Copy these words. The dot reminds you when to use a touch join.

encounter flattened studying decoded equipment

saucer secrets landings binary advanced

messages ground images sending weather

Add a dot to indicate the touch joins in each word, then copy the words.

cause search planet explain claimed

increase feature sightings human images

liquid conspiracy geometric formation artistic

Self-assessment: Touch joins

Copy the text. Remember to be careful with your touch joins.

The Easter Island statues, or moai, make a stunning sight when seen for the first time. Some soar over 10 metres high, facing inland even though they are located close to the brilliant, aquamarine sea. All have long heads with long ears, and long upper torsos. The statues have their arms placed along their bodies or resting on their stomachs. There are some with eyes. The eyes are made of white and red stone and coral. A few wear hats made from scoria, a volcanic stone.

Self-assessment

Rate your touch joins.

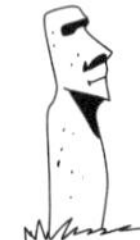

☐ Good.

☐ Very good.

☐ Excellent!

Horizontal joins

Joins from b, o, r, v and w have a slight dip. Be careful not to dip too far.

Copy these letter pairs.

bi br bu by oi om or on ri rn rm

ru wi wr wn wm wu vi vu vy

og

Remember: when joining horizontally to a, c, d, g, o or q, some retracing is required.

Copy these words with horizontal joins.

mysterious Bigfoot known forests northwest across

throughout covered living bulldozer report wooden

however phenomenon snowmen footprints turned

monster bipedal describe dwelling wilderness stories

Underline the letter pairs in the words below that will have a horizontal join when written in cursive. Prove your answers by writing all the words in cursive.

ground brought tourist loch proof survived

evidence encountered European elongated royal

ISBN: 9780170424080

Horizontal joins to 'e'

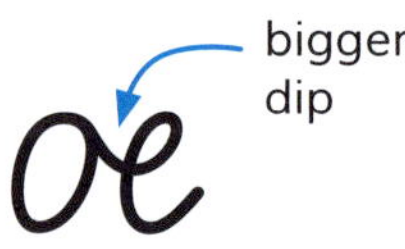

Remember: when making a horizontal join to 'e', increase the size of the dip.

Copy these words, then underline each horizontal join to 'e'.

creak went believe never remembered crew above

poem reconstruct represent realistic departure nerve

attractive massive extensive aggressive shoes canoe

poetry week allowed diverse convenience event

Rewrite these words in cursive, then underline your neatest horizontal join to 'e'.

tower echoed occurred tomatoes does disappeared

bureau creature enquire furore fluorescent fireworks

firewall fixture respect distress declared compared

drover relax superpower sweet everlasting readily

Copy the text. Remember to take care with your horizontal joins to 'e'.

An unexplained mystery is a very unusual event that cannot readily be explained by science or reason.

ISBN: 9780170424080

Horizontal joins to 's'

Remember: when joining horizontally to 's' the shape of the 's' doesn't change.

rs

Make a careful horizontal sweep, then retrace the top of 's'.

Copy these letter pairs.

bs fs os rs us ws bs fs os rs us ws

Copy the text. Underline the horizontal joins to 's'.

When the newsroom reports on the prospect of a mystery, I absolutely believe! Many explorers defeat obstacles to observe evidence and test their beliefs. Even when evidence is sparse, they report their findings on websites and obsess over sightings of meteors or ghosts or unexplained hollows in the snow. While we may not have photos or fossils to prove these sightings are real, their existence is no less real to me than rainbows or dinosaurs!

get.ga/PMWA193

Horizontal joins and speed loops

Make a smooth upsweeping motion, before looping to the ascender. The loop crosses at the height of a body letter.

Copy these letter pairs.

bh bk bl ob oh ok ol rb rh rk rl wb

wh wk wl rh bh bk bl ob

Copy these words, being careful with your horizontal joins to speed loops.

scholar isolation volcanic prohibit noble book

Copy the text. Pay careful attention to your horizontal joins to speed loops.

Many books have been written by scholars who have

investigated mysterious happenings. Sometimes, an

unusual event is thought to be a trick to fool others.

At other times, even after a thorough investigation

the mystery is not able to be satisfactorily solved.

Horizontal joins from 'f'

When joining from 'f', lift your pen and use the crossbar to join to the next letter.

Copy.

fa fe fi fl fo fu fr fs ft fy

flying flock false factual famous surface

scientific confirm reflection demystify classify

fe

Remember: lower the crossbar to join from 'f' to 'e'.

Copy.

feat fearless fever feeling feast fern feud

fo

Remember: retrace across the top of 'o' when joining from 'f' to 'o'.

Copy.

fossil footprint force found forest formation

ISBN: 9780170424080

Self-assessment: Horizontal joins

Copy the text. Remember to be careful with your horizontal joins.

Amelia Earhart was an American aviator who became
the first woman to fly solo across the Atlantic Ocean.
Years later, during her extremely courageous attempt to
fly around the world, this famous pilot vanished over
the Central Pacific Ocean. Earhart was a well-known
figure, and her disappearance led to a full-scale search
for her location. Earhart and her famous plane were
never found. Eventually, all possibilities were exhausted,
and the many books written by scholars on her
disappearance could not reach a conclusion. Earhart
has served as an inspiration for young pilots.

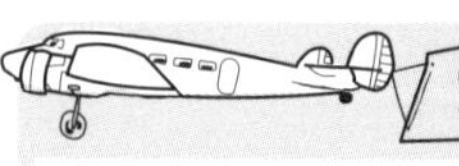

Self-assessment

Rate your horizontal joins.

☐ Good.

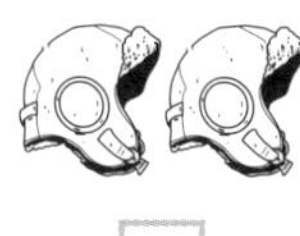

☐ Very good.

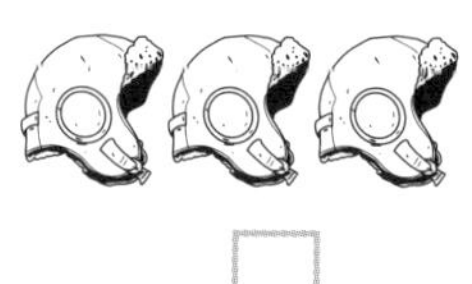

☐ Excellent!

ISBN: 9780170424080

Slope

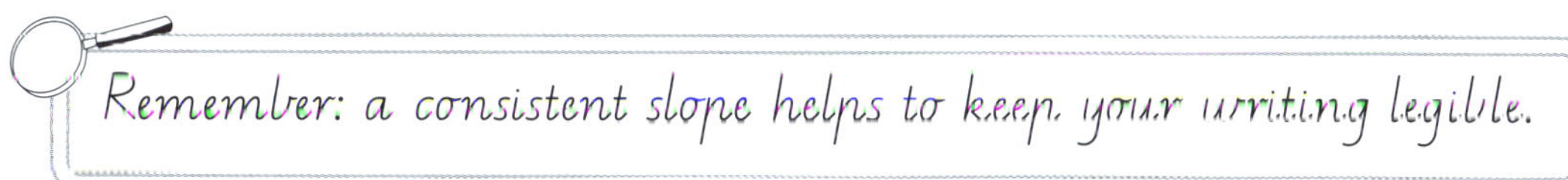

Write the letters of the alphabet against the slope lines.

a b c

Write the letters of the alphabet, then check your slope by drawing in the slope lines using a ruler.

Copy the text, then check your slope. Choose 10 words and use a ruler to draw in the slope lines.

Stonehenge is located in Wiltshire, England, near the
town of Amesbury. It is a stark ring of standing stones.
The stones are about 4 metres high and 2 metres wide.
Archaeologists have calculated that the structure is over
5000 years old. There are many theories as to why and
how it was built. Today, the area is roped off to prevent
people from touching the stones and damaging them.

get.ga/PMWA194

ISBN: 9780170424080

Spacing

Remember: correct spacing between letters and words helps with legibility.

Rewrite the text, correcting the spacing.

Ea ster Island, or Rapa Nu i, is a small pi ece of land in the South Pacific. The island is famous for its 900 huge huma n-like statu e s, or moai. The s tatues were carved hundreds of years ago byRapa Nui artists. How the statues we re moved remains a mystery.

Copy these words in the spaces provided. How does your handwriting vary in size from the models?

Rapa Nui construction moai unknown hilly

Polynesian tourism village anchor ancestry

Circle the word in each pair with the most appropriate spacing.

ca r v ed carved p latfor ms platforms famous famous

ISBN: 9780170424080

Size

Gradually increase the size of the pattern while maintaining your accuracy.

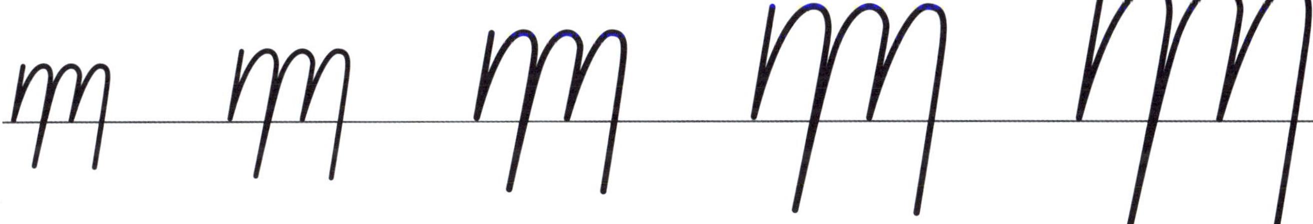

Copy the words. Can you change the size of your writing and maintain your legibility?

disappear disappear disappear

ship ship ship ship ship

Circle a word in the size you found most comfortable to write. Underline your most legible word.

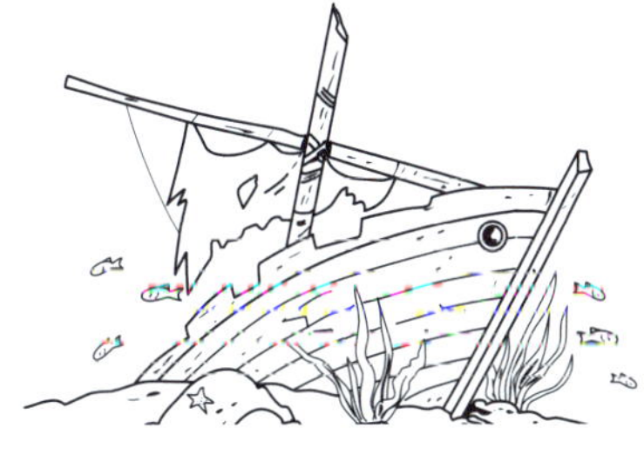

ISBN: 9780170424080

Copy the text. Take special care with your slope, spacing and size.

The Bermuda Triangle is an area where many mysterious incidents have occurred. Dozens of ships, planes and people have disappeared under strange circumstances with no good explanation. The triangle is located off the east coast of Mexico and the United States of America, in the Atlantic Ocean. The three points of the triangle are the cities of Miami and San Juan, and the island of Bermuda.

Peer review

Ask your partner to give you some feedback on how well you wrote the text above.
Ask them to notice how legible your handwriting is.

2 stars (two things you did well)

1 wish (a way for you to improve)

Unjoined letters

Revise your unjoined letters.

a b c d e f g h i j k l m n o p q r s t u v w x y z

Convert the following words from cursive to unjoined letters.

Cursive	Unjoined
triangle	
located	
Atlantic	
mysteriously	
disappeared	
Bermuda	

Copy the text.

People began telling stories about the triangle of sea between the islands of Bermuda and Puerto Rico and the city of Miami where planes and boats made an abrupt disappearance. Some people were filled with doubt and said that the idea of a mystery triangle must be phoney. Others believed some strange force must be at work.

ISBN: 9780170424080

Patterning exercises

Copy this diagram of Stonehenge as accurately as possible, using the circle as a guide.

Capital letters

Revise your capital letters.

A B C D E F G H I J K L M N O P

Q R S T U V W X Y Z

Pilots use a two-letter code to abbreviate the names of countries when navigating. Copy these country names and their abbreviations.

Country	Code	Country	Code
Australia	AU	Pakistan	PK
Indonesia	ID	United States of America	US
Thailand	TH	France	FR
Papua New Guinea	PG	Puerto Rico	PR
Mexico	MX	Canada	CA
Ireland	IE	Suriname	SR
Senegal	SN	Sudan	SD

ISBN: 9780170424080

Numerals

Copy each distance in numerals and words.

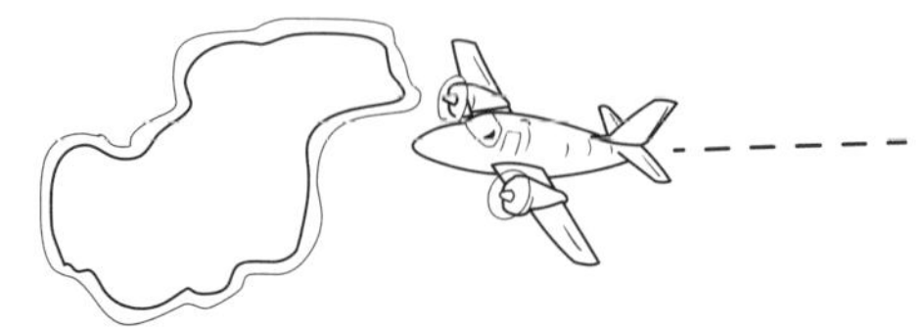

Distances flown by Amelia Earhart on her final journey

Miami to San Juan	1660 km one thousand, six hundred and sixty kilometres
San Juan to Caripito	983 km nine hundred and eighty-three kilometres
Caripito to Paramaribo	989 km nine hundred and eighty-nine kilometres
Paramaribo to Natal	2567 km two thousand, five hundred and sixty-seven kilometres
Natal to St Louis	7499 km seven thousand, four hundred and ninety-nine kilometres

How many kilometres did Amelia Earhart fly to get from Miami to Caripito?

ISBN: 9780170424080

Punctuation

Rewrite these sentences, using correct punctuation and capital letters where required.

bigfoot is a legendary ape-like beast rumoured to dwell in the forests of the pacific northwest in the usa. in october 1967, two men believed they had discovered the footprints of bigfoot in california, usa

the yeti is a mythical human-like creature thought to exist in the snowy himalayan mountains, in the countries of tibet and nepal a movie called 'the abominable snowman' is based on the legend of the yeti

loch ness, home to the mythical loch ness monster, is a large freshwater lake located in scotland in 1934, british newspaper 'the daily mail' published a now-famous photograph of what looked like the loch ness monster

ISBN: 9780170424080

Double letter combinations

oss

When double 's' comes after a horizontal join, modify the second 's'.

ess

When double 's' comes after a diagonal join, both letters are modified.

get.ga/PMWA195

Copy these words, being careful to write your double 's' joins correctly.

eeriness obsess glasses Loch Ness awareness classify

toss gloss floss across boss gross albatross moss

In high school, students are often asked to find the key words (most important words) in non-fiction texts. Copy the text below, being careful with both types of double 's' joins, then use a coloured pencil to underline the key words.

In 1933, a husband and wife asserted that they had seen a massive whale-like creature across the water in the lake at Inverness. This was the beginning of countless modern stories of the Loch Ness monster.

Crossing double 't' will speed up your handwriting.

tt tt

Cross double 't' with one stroke or two.

butter butter bottle bottle kitten kitten little little

offer

When writing double 'f', extend the crossbar of the first 'f' upwards to make a loop for the second 'f'. Lift your pen or pencil before adding the crossbar

Copy these words with double 'f'.

offers differentiating difference effect suffice

affect coffee effort unofficial toffee bluff

office staff whiff puff stiff standoff sheriff

Copy the text.

Unsolved mysteries can affect people in different ways. Investigators set off in search of evidence to affirm their theories, but it can be difficult to find sufficient proof and they are often left baffled. When the official search is over, some investigators will continue searching for the truth for years. Others simply brush off the case as a mystery and affix their attention to their next one.

ISBN: 9780170424080

Copy the text, paying close attention to words with double letters.

It is believed a rip tide played a part in Prime Minister Harold Holt's disappearance in 1967. Rips are our silent beach killers, as many swimmers don't know how to identify them. Rips are strong currents that start near the shore and flow out to sea. The rip area often appears calmer and darker. Usually there is no wave activity, which can utterly deceive swimmers into thinking that it is a safe place to swim. Our surf lifesavers can read surf conditions and set up the red and yellow flags indicating a safe place to swim. The best advice, if you happen to get caught in a rip, is to not panic, try to float and raise your hand to indicate you require assistance.

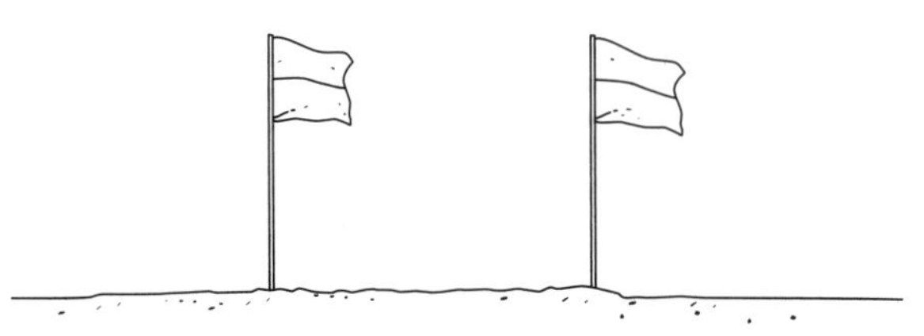

ISBN: 9780170424080

Converting between scripts

Convert these words from cursive to unjoined letters.

Cursive	Unjoined
Australia	
vanished	
surf	
recovered	
theories	
explained	
lowered	
swimming	
mysterious	

Convert this text from unjoined letters to cursive.

Harold Holt was Prime Minister of Australia from

January 1966 until his mysterious disappearance in late

1967. Holt vanished while swimming in the surf on the

morning of 17 December 1967 at Cheviot Beach, near

Portsea in Victoria. His body was never recovered. While

there are many theories about how Holt disappeared, it's

likely that he simply drowned. The Australian flag was

lowered to half-mast to express mourning for his loss.

Print script: Labelling maps

Remember: print script can be used for labelling maps, graphs, charts and diagrams, as well as writing headings and addressing envelopes.

Add labels to the map using print script. Remember to use all capitals for country names.

United States of America | Cuba | Miami
Florida | San Juan | Puerto Rico | Bermuda

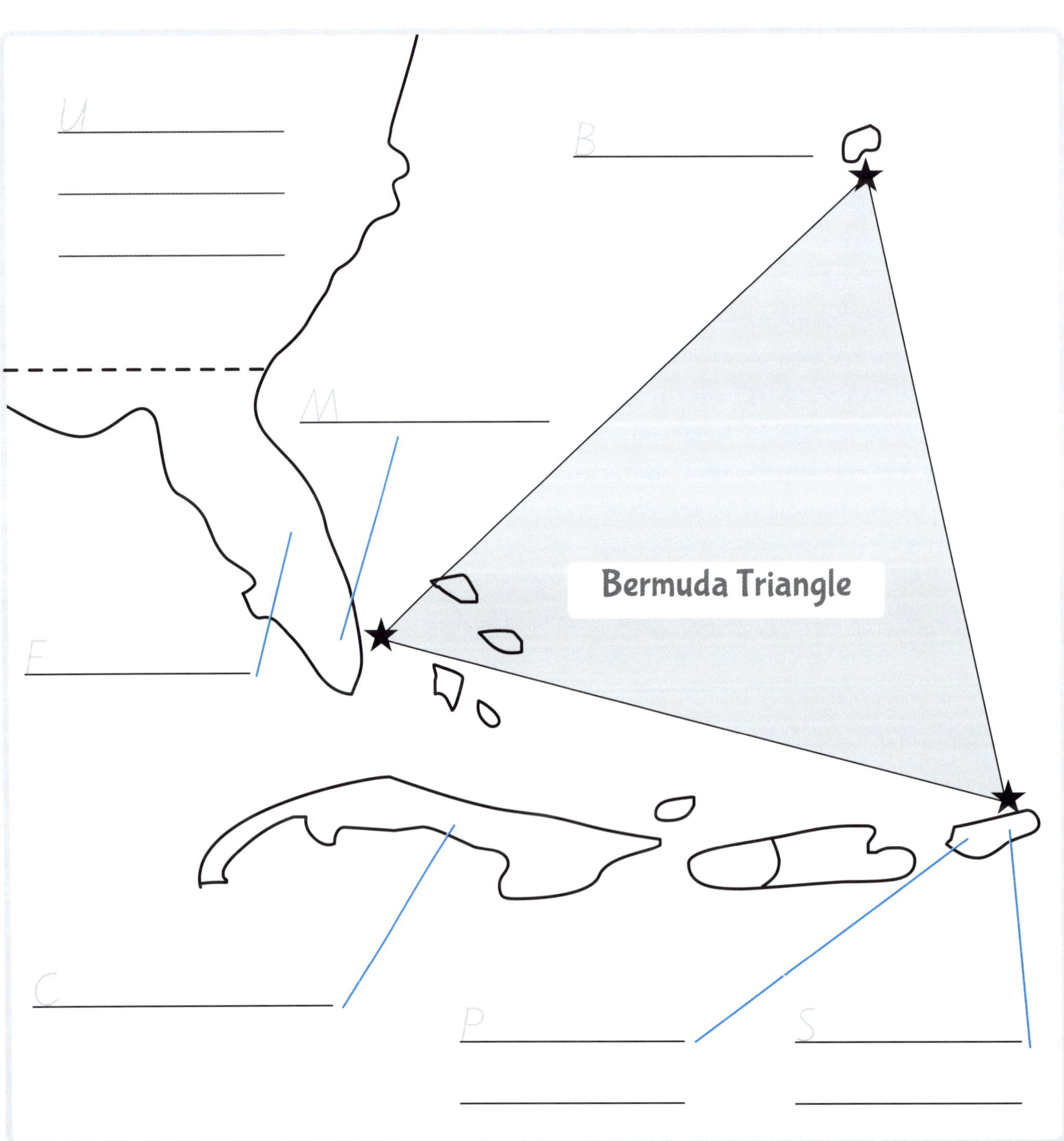

Print script: Labelling diagrams

Add labels to the diagram. Use print script.

Amelia Earhart's Lockheed model 10 Electra plane

1. landing light
2. fuel tank
3. sun blinds
4. thermometer
5. pull-up cable
6. rear cockpit

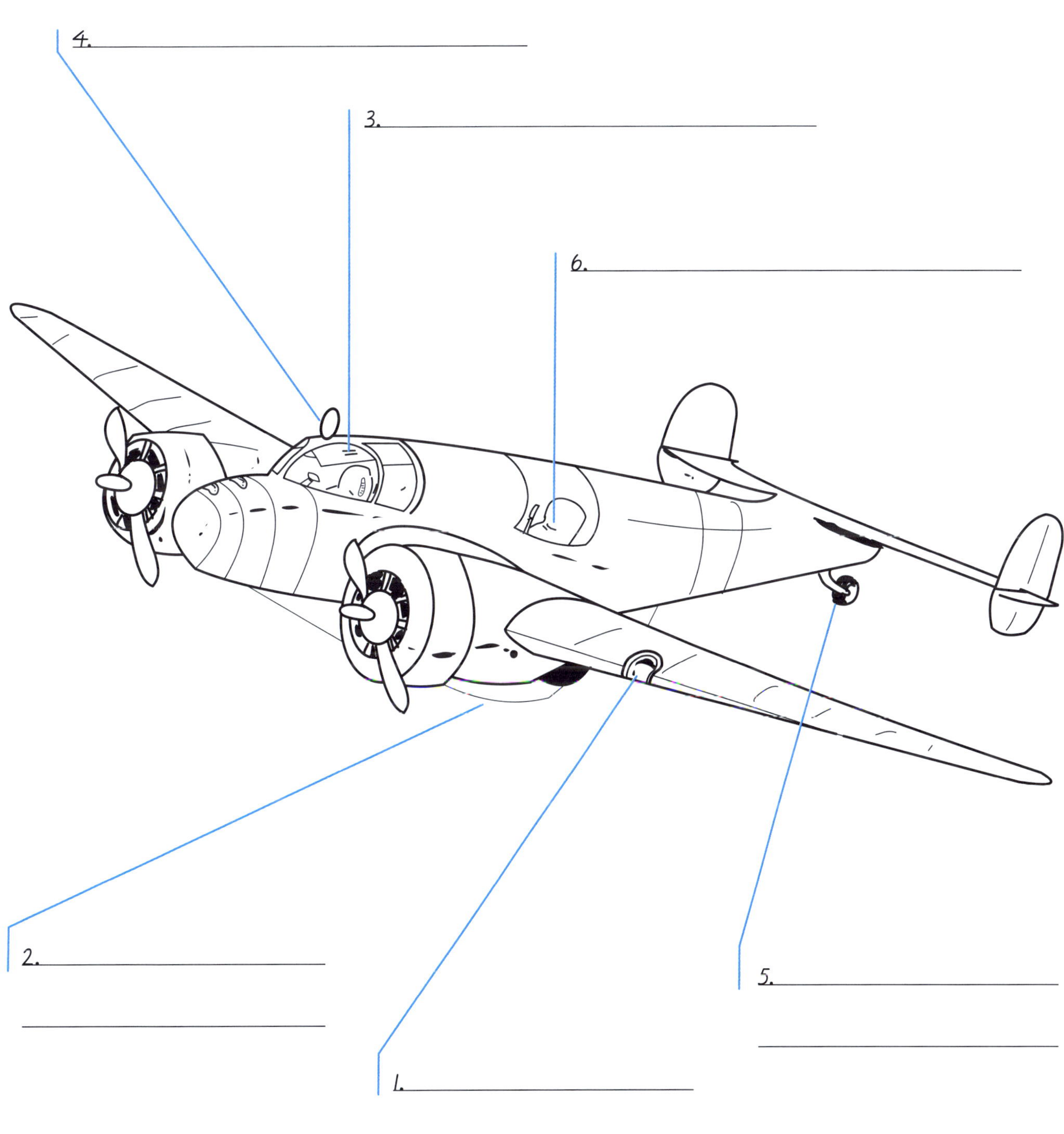

ISBN: 9780170424080

Print script: Labelling timelines

Add the events from the box to the timeline below, using print script.

1915 A pilot fires on a UFO over London.

1947 A UFO crashes in Roswell, New Mexico, in the USA.

1952 Six discs circle above a town in Argentina.

1966 A UFO hovers above Westall High School, Melbourne.

2006 A saucer-shaped craft hovers above O'Hare Airport, USA.

Timeline of famous UFO sightings

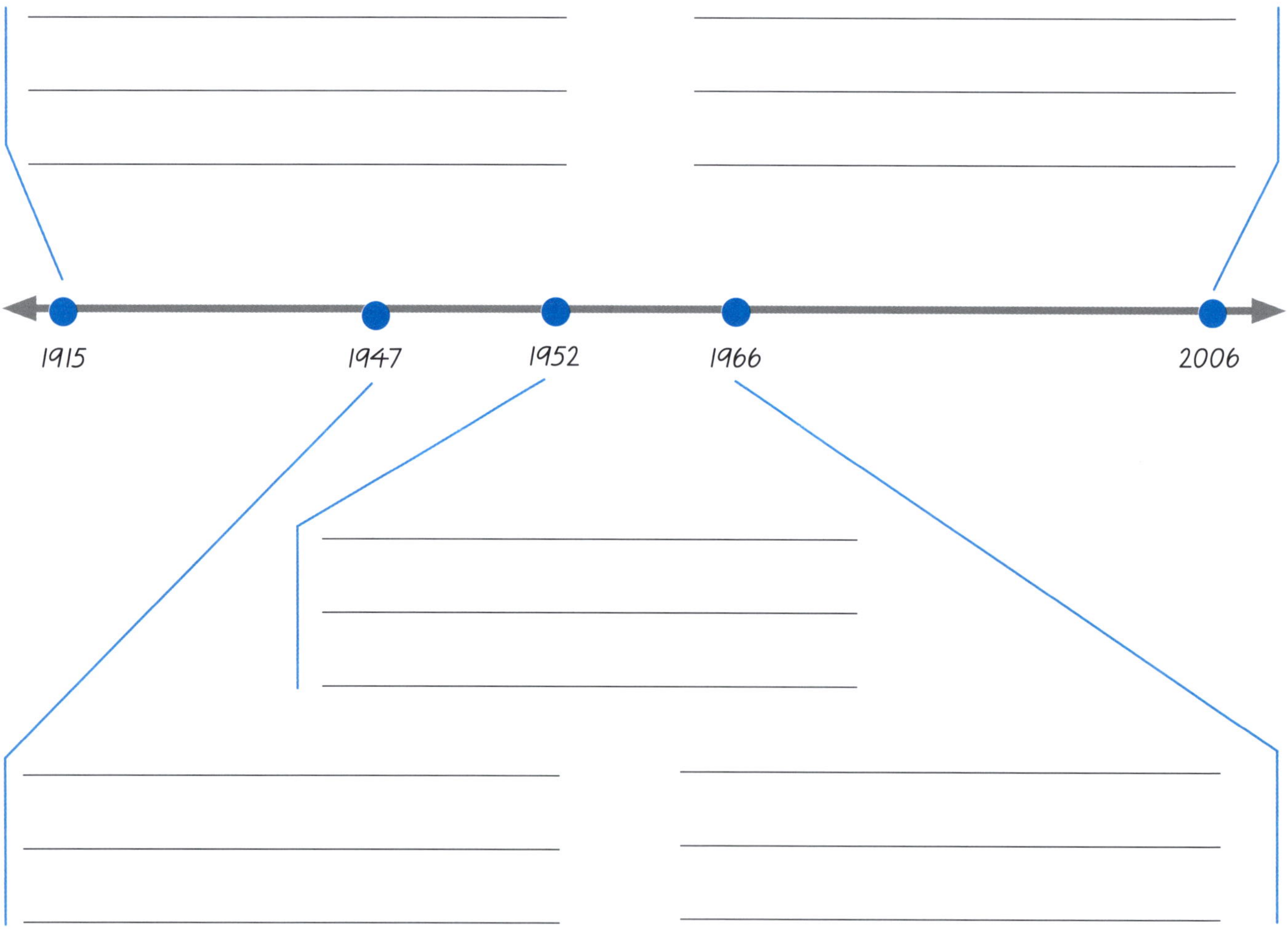

1915 1947 1952 1966 2006

ISBN: 9780170424080

Using pen lifts

Lifting your pen at the appropriate time, such as when you make a touch join, will help you to move your hand comfortably across the page as you write.

Practise using frequent pen lifts. Copy the text.

Prime Minister Harold Holt was at the beach with friends. While they chose to laze on the sand, he went swimming alone and disappeared. As he was an agile and capable athlete, many people did not believe that he had drowned. One answer to this mystery was that he faked his own death. Another was that he was abducted by enemy sailors in a submarine. The prime minister had a shoulder injury when he disappeared. As the beach where he swam was well known for having giant swells, it is plausible that he was washed out to sea by a swell.

ISBN: 9780170424080

Legibility: Slope

Practise maintaining a consistent slope. Copy each word in the slope grid.

mystery

disappear

life

career

identity

records

attempt

theories

ISBN: 9780170424080

Legibility: Spacing

Copy the text, then check your spacing. Colour a small square between each word.

Amelia Earhart is best known as the first female pilot to fly across the Atlantic Ocean. Earhart was born in Kansas, USA, on 24 July 1897. In June 1937, she departed from Miami, Florida, with her navigator Fred Noonan. They planned to fly around the world. They mysteriously disappeared while flying over the Pacific Ocean, from Lae in New Guinea towards Howland Island. Amelia Earhart was last heard from on 2 July 1937. Amelia, her navigator and her plane were never found.

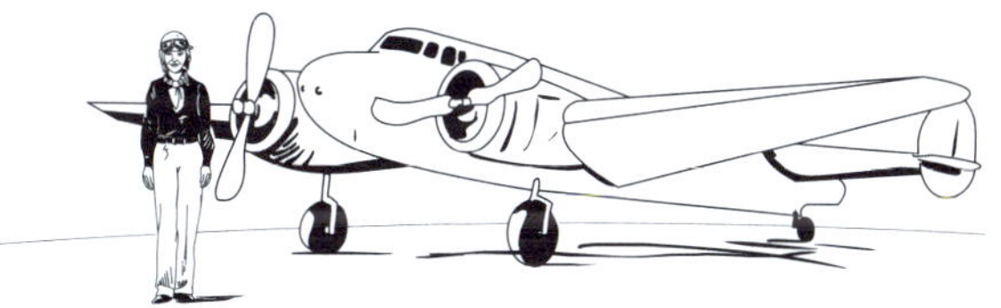

get.ga/PMWA196

Rewrite these words with more appropriate spacing between the letters.

av ia tor rec ords p ilot in str ument dep artures

sig nals p osition dis coveries m e moir attempt p lane

ISBN: 9780170424080

Legibility: Size

Copy the words. Can you change the size of your writing and maintain your legibility?

never never never never

tides tides tides tides tides

Circle a word above in the size you found the most comfortable to write.
Underline your most legible word.

How many times can you fit the words below along the lines with no space between the words?

waves

_____ times

accidental

_____ times

gone

_____ times

mourning

_____ times

swimming

_____ times

Speed and legibility

Work with a partner. How many times can you write the word 'mystery' in cursive in one minute?

Now write the word again. This time, write as neatly as you can, using cursive. How many times did you write it in one minute?

______ times

Now find out how many times you can write the word neatly using unjoined letters in one minute.

______ times

My fastest script:

______ times

My neatest script:

My preferred script:

Handwriting in context

Should mysteries always be solved? Complete the PMI chart on this topic in your neatest handwriting. Make sure you pay careful attention to the slope, spacing and size of your handwriting, and to all your letter joins.

- In the Plus section, write what is positive about mysteries being solved.
- In the Minus section, write what is negative about mysteries being solved.
- In the Interesting section, write what is interesting about solving mysteries.

Plus
Minus
Interesting

Reflective writing activity

Your years of primary school are nearly over and high school is just around the corner. Use the space below to reflect on the past seven years of primary school. What are your first memories? Which teachers and classmates, and which learning, sporting or creative activities have been important to you? Your response could be in the form of a narrative, a poem, a letter or anything you like. Make sure you pay careful attention to the slope, spacing and size of your handwriting, and to all your letter joins.

Draw yourself on your first day of primary school.

Draw yourself now.

Teacher observation guide

Student is: left-handed ☐ right-handed ☐

Student demonstrates correct posture, paper position and pencil grip. ☐

Student forms the Victorian Modern Cursive alphabet with accuracy. ☐

Student forms capital letters with accuracy. ☐

Student forms numerals with accuracy. ☐

Student forms the following joins with accuracy:

- speed loops ☐
- diagonal joins ☐
- touch joins ☐
- horizontal joins ☐

Student can convert between scripts. ☐

Student uses 9 mm regular writing lines with accuracy. ☐

Student has an understanding of the factors that influence legibility (slope, spacing, size, speed). ☐

Student uses Victorian Modern Cursive cursive confidently. ☐

Student is progressing towards a fluent and legible personal handwriting style. ☐

Notes:

....

....

....

Date:

....